Augmented Seventh

by

Gwyneth Hughes

© Gwyneth Hughes

Chapbook series published by:

Pipers' Ash Limited

www.supamasu.com

CHIPPENHAM ◆ WILTSHIRE ◆ ENGLAND
SN15 4BW

Acknowledgments

Unhallowed appeared in *The Frogmore Papers*
Bowling appeared in *Outposts*
Elegy Four appeared in *Psychopoetica*
Leading Lady appeared in *Beyond The Boundaries*
Fleeting appeared in *Writing Women*
Lingam appeared in *Headlock*
Maternity appeared in *Weyfarers*
Holla appeared in *Voyage*
Elegy Three and Come appeared in *Target*
Libido and Ruminant appeared in *Fatchance*
By Any Other and Side Light appeared in *Pennine Platform*
Observance, God's Acre, and Deposit appeared in *Staple*
Appetite, Reign, Advertisement, and Guilt Trip
appeared in *Poetry Nottingham*
Elegy One, Impatience, Bouquet, and In High Feather appeared in *Iota*
Elegy Two, Polarity, Celibacy, Fall, and Reunion appeared in *Orbis*
Da Capo, Chronic, Triplicity, Spaceites, Repose, Nostalgia,
End Of The Line, and Pervasion appeared in *The Cardiff Poet*
Revelation, Family Portrait Two and Four, Wandering, Litter,
Bearings, and Encounter appeared in *Envoi*

'Salisbury Edition'
ISBN 1-902628-18-7

Contents

Do is for Daughter
1. Fleeting
2. Observance
3. Mummies
4. Triplicity
5. Revelation
6. Brood
7. Ascendancy

Re is for Sister
8. Family Portrait
9. Six Elegies
10. Reunion

Mi is for Lover
11. Impatience
12. Appetite
13. Bowling
14. Bouquet
15. Scant
16. Perfidy
17. Link
18. Lingam
19. Wandering
20. Pervasion
21. Come
22. End Of The Line
23. Fall

Fa is for Mother
24. Free Choice
25. Fragrance
26. In High Feather
27. Reign
28. Maternity
29. Diapason
30. Heredity

Sol is for Survivor
31. Celibacy
32. Libido
33. Litter
34. A Meteorite
35. Via
36. Da Capo
37. Asunder
38. Ruminant
39. Repose
40. God's Acre

La is for Singer
41. Summit
42. Chronic
43. In Command
44. Bearings
45. Polarity
46. Encounter
47. Unhallow
48. Leading Lady
49. Token
50. Joy After Pain

Si is for Spectator
51. Carolyn's Account
52. By Any Other
53. Holla
54. Side Light
55. Advertisement
56. Guilt Trip
57. Spaceites
58. Aloof
59. Radicals
60. Deposit
61. Crypt
62. Nostalgia

Do is for Daughter

1   Fleeting

she opened her eyes and smiled
I smiled back
but turned my head
to lay my book aside
then looked again
into her eyes
kissed the hand
clasped in mine for hours
as I'd sat there
reading a little
but mostly thinking of the past
praying she'd awaken

and now she had
she recognized me
without a doubt
and pulled my hand
against her own parched lips
then closed her eyes once more
in sleep
her final sleep
while I cursed myself
for the instant I had lost
in setting my book
on the hospital table

2   Observance

I assumed I had time
no one had warned me
rigor mortis sets in so soon
I thought I could wait to close your eyes
prolong communion
thankful we were alone in the hospital room

you stretched in crimson mud
me leaning forward
gazing into green pools
where hazel reeds encircled black pupils
tunnels to your soul
I wanted to keep open

then the nurse came in
and put her fingers on your lids
too late to seal them
how long had I sat entranced
in that luxuriant region
I'd never wander through again?

strangers swarmed around
in silence I prayed you didn't mind
and were perhaps even journeying on
as curious and defiant as you had lived
entering eternity
wide-eyed

3   Mummies

like large puppets on the ground
preserved from decay
by odd conditions of the air
in the crypt of an ancient church

a velvet knight a valiant crusader
and his satin wife
laid side by side
each with twisted thighs and forearms crossed

but illuminated by a torch
the guide points out
how their worn knuckles shine
from tourists like us groping for good luck

"Where did the piece of stocking go
once in the place where the hole is now?"
I kneel as Mother shows me
fluff under the bed

this couple has been dead for centuries
corpses on a cold stone floor
"You'll get locked in"
calls my husband from the exit

I bend to touch the lady's hand
stroke her smooth hard fingers
then hurry on to join the group
huddled in daylight glare

thinking of my mother
who now drifts in cotton clouds
"It turned to dust, balls of dust
nothing to be afraid of"

4 Triplicity

I lay between them
he on one side
she on the other
as they embraced
each one kissing me
unaware of the mistake

her hands touched my throat
his hands caressed my chest
her hands stroked my back
his hands moved under my waist
he believed she surrendered
she thought he obeyed

but both were only loving me
and I was slyly laughing
as I sprawled in the middle
one against each leg
and held them separate
my pleasure double in their place

until he whispered
"tell me I'm a genius"
and she murmured
"tell me I'm a saint"
then I arose and killed the two of them
and bound their remains

hip to hip
breast to breast
mouth to mouth
to bury them that way
and consequently hug myself to death
on top of their grave

5 Revelation

the great white mare
moves down the steep rocky trail before me
and the brusque movement of strong wide haunches
shakes the velvet edges of a long dark vulva
revealed on each switch of her tail

my father walks before her
holding the reins
close to her jerking snorting nostrils
guiding her forward in a voice
both gentle and stern
the burden on her back
tilting left toward a somber ravine
or right to rub large lumps of clear brown clay
from the flank of the mountain rising round and high

and I understand my origin
child of this gaunt nervous
poorly-shaven man
and his husky horse
filly of distant blood-red stars
seen often descending the evening sky
with a cautious clumsy stride
a human phallus thrust between the midnight folds
of rippling silk and she gave birth

then weak awkward foal I stood
between the hind legs of my mother
under the vertical black genital wreath
that crowned me queen of the earth
and daughter of an animal heaven

6   Brood

tears dormant
swallowed long ago
from incubation
in the moss of my brain
suddenly today
broke their shells
and swarmed out in solemn rows

from the cave of my throat
rang one name
their incantation
amplified
to a clamorous chorus
they sang remorse
until hoarse and hissing

love's inundation
burst from a nest
of what once seemed hate
after so many silent years
how can grief
as old as this
bring me such solace?

7 Ascendancy

As soon as I heard his voice I knew him,
father I had never seen
but whose words had resounded
through the somber vault of my mother's womb.

As soon as he spoke, I understood
my vagabond father had returned
to the cavern of my conception
after millenniums of absence.

She rose resplendent to greet him,
her scarlet veils fluttering over and around
his coarse brown cape and hood,
and led him to rest in her abandoned bed,

then went out to perform her duties,
queen of the day,
while my weary earth father lay back and slept
on the perfumed furs of her opulent couch.

When she returned at twilight,
she found father and daughter enlaced.
He, cold. Me, princess of the night,
pale replica of my radiant mother,

I transferred his granite body to her mourning arms
and emerged, sinister, triumphant,
the skirt of my silver gown now soiled
and spotted in crimson.

Re is for Sister

8   Family Portrait

Him
Not a word he said -
only animal noises
as with bowed head
I jumbled wisdom
to jungle calls.

Rhinoceros or crocodile,
orangutan or hyena,
lions, tigers, panthers,
ferocious bears -
sense shuffled from experience,

until he'd stop and say,
"you can go play now"
and all the angry beasts
sprawling on his chest
turned to devour him.

              **

Everything he touched
turned to dust,
King Midas in reverse,

but no Pactolus
washed the jinx
nor could the Styx

end cataclysm.
Anti-Midas came,
phantom father,

later,
roach of hate,
black coachman,
to drive my brother's hearse.

Her

"A pill," she'd say
with arrogance
when we were little.
"Like an old Eskimo
dropping off the sled
into the midnight snow,
I'll never be a burden
to myself
or to my children.
I'll know when my time comes
and leave with dignity
on my own two feet."

Now she sits in a rocking chair,
her body weak,
but with indomitable pride intact,
convinced it isn't courage that she lacks
upon the brink,
admitting no more terror of remission
than she did a debt of faith.
The unlocked door never opened,
pills never bought,
she babbles on about her only tragedy:
the splendid son who -
inconceivably -
took his own life.

Me

If I went back
to our dirty house
on our noisy street,
what would I find?
Kitchen foes still shouting
up the dark refuge stairs
where we tore wallpaper ribbons,
giggling as we passed,
and in the hall
by the telephone,
the sardonic joke your jack-knife
gouged out of grey plaster:
HOME SWEET HOME?

I did come back.
The building is gone.
The place where it stood
is a parking lot now.
I stroll on the asphalt
paving our old yard
and remember our laughter.
We took their hatred in our stride,
shrugged off hardship,
went about our ways,
until decades later
your suicide
surprised the others.

You
Your pain broke at the bottom of a wall
and all of us were hit by it,
shrapnel shooting your despair
straight into the hearts of the survivors.

When half-way down did you repent
to shackle us in your scrap iron,
howl and thrash to halt explosion,
review our faces on the rising pavement

or swoop, egocentric swallow,
plunging mute into oblivion
that opened under the asphalt
where universal sorrow was destroyed?

Us
Put ancient grief into a heap
and set fire to the lot.
Watch old misery feed the flames.
There's no way to again be happy
if you keep looking back.

Drop past chagrin into a trash bin
and let it go to rot.
View the insects dragging vivid
fragments off until the scenes
scurry to smithereens.

Throw nostalgia in the sea.
You'll never find the spot
where it will settle under brine,
no shrine, no tomb, no memorandum,
registered in sand.

Heave your history from a cliff
and grant it lie forgotten,
bits of broken ego earth,
worn anonymous under rain
to clay of commonplace pain.

9   Six Elegies

Supersonic
if I could scream sufficiently
long and loud
gates would open
under graveyard grass

if I could cry
sharp enough in pitch
I'd shatter chains of death
where you hang caught

then through marble barriers
you'd push
your vigorous way
no more a hostage

liberated
by one strident note of pain
if I could only shriek
what I feel

Haunt
are you still here
beneath the surface
beyond the rim
wakened from sleep
by my weeping?

still close by
listening to my voice
whisper your name
kept near the wall
by my calling?

behind the curtain
of harsh sunshine?
I'll only know
when I in turn
watch others cry

Keepsakes

why didn't I steal more?
every worldly vision crushed to beads
everything you ever were or wanted
caught in globes that I could hold
rosary of souvenirs

instead I took some pencils from a drawer
books and photographs
a handkerchief a belt
and now have only light things left
to counterweight your absent heaviness

Dichotomy

whenever a jet plane
streaks the sky
rows of a distant graveyard
rise in my mind

when noticing slight things
you would have liked
my eyes and ears
relay the sounds the sights

thinking of you
I heave deep sighs
breathing for two
while half my heart
pumps you alive

Stark

It was simple when sorrow veiled the wall
and everywhere was soft in shadow
until dawn broke the velvet fog
and screamed on the horizon
Bleaching rays of day
hammered grief down
to a narrow black grimace
And in the hot glare of high noon
the doorway to my respite of cool weeping
stabs a rictus crack across a flat façade

Acceptance
I unwind the hands of every dial
but no matter how hard
I shovel time back
it augments its gravel hindrance.

The pebble past accumulates
hour upon hour
though I roll away great stone days
from the quarry of our severance.

High on your plateau
without lifting a granite finger
you lie scornful of my struggle
for your deliverance,

until the final boulder falls
and I sit in a green meadow
and gaze on a purple mountain
of remembrance.

Then your death too
takes its compact place,
peak along a ridge of bereavement,
crest on a distant range of sufferance.

10 Reunion

I took her ashes to his grave
and propped the box against the tomb
then left them in the sun and silence

knowing perfectly well it was absurd
that she was only cinders and he bones
and that no spirits whispered there behind me

strolling out of earshot. Then I returned
and kneeled in the wet grass and kissed the stone
and put her plastic coffin in my satchel

my fingers in his hollow name
and said, "we three, again, alone,"
and left, the rucksack on my shoulder

Mi is for Lover

11 Impatience

as a spider in a web
awaits a fly
as a cow yearns
to be milked
my ear open
for the knelling of your voice
announcing vespers

leaves in a dry wind
expecting rain
arch their bellies to heaven
and whine and toss
I await you
as grass billows
beneath a horse's teeth

the way the surf
withdraws from rocks
before a tidal wave
the way snow packs
a jagged crater mouth
before the uproar
of an avalanche

12 Appetite

ripe orange of an instant
peel split to a pout
pulp of dreams and laughter
all the lessons all the thoughts

gush past the pressure
of my lips through my kiss
until I've sucked you flat
swallowed each membrane wish

turned you inside out
to gnaw you to a rind
drop you on the ground
go on, esurient child

licking palms and fingers
for the last stray remnants
of your sweet orange mind
emptied of its essence

13 Bowling

the ball of your head
heaved down the alley
to where the future stands
in a fan of eventuality

and the nine skittles of fate
rub tummies as they fall
roll bounce and are swept off
except this exact instant

tottering on its base
then reaching balance stability
erect and arrogant
under my fingers

14 Bouquet

rose men now
leaf arms raised above
thick blossom heads
naked and knee deep
in the glass bowl of my skull

hot house lovers
feet clipped on a bias off
suck up
stagnant reminiscence
through stiff hollow stalks

three flowers
artificially alive
rows of phallic thorns
protrude
and prick blood from my fingers

15 Scant

the past is a jigsaw puzzle
with one piece missing
the negative of an old photograph
hung over today's vision

an image in a discarded magazine
faded tattered
bits of an ancient statue
assembled in a museum

the hole shows your silhouette
the snapshot seized you in youth
I edited the revue
and am now guardian of relics

16 Perfidy

from esophagus to coccyx
the calyx of a heart
unfolds its corolla
to an evening everglade
where sweet lagoons
bleak and smooth
lie heavy for a victim

some creature will be caught
in this dark honey
pool of carnivorous love
seeping through the marshland
of a pulse
and the coronary petal
will close upon a prey

tiny insect
little bug
you buzz happy affection
in the hilarious light of morning
before the iris of my sundew eyes
wide open
and innocent

17 Link

Your balls
in gentle candlelight
dangle like plump figs
between your thighs
as you bend over for underwear
cast earlier in frenzy on the floor.

From my vantage point,
still reclining on our mattress,
I'm reminded of the great stone lion
who overhead
stalks the ornate parapet
in town.

Each time I passed,
patriarchal library books
loading my arms,
I'd pause to slyly contemplate
his graceful stucco testicles
between taut haunches.

Full of admiration,
then as now,
wishing to retain you by one ankle,
I scrutinize your scrotum
from behind.
But alas, you rise and turn.

So I divert my eyes
the way I'd shift my gaze
with genteel breeding
from his masculine anatomy
and trudge across the bridge
in demure haste.

18 Lingam

an old man in a train
pulling his coat open
at the entrance to a tunnel

a young man standing on a crowded bus
pelvis pressed
to a seated woman's shoulder

while she reads on
like the impervious nibbling hens
among strutting cooing male pigeons

before a bench
where adolescent boys
raucously exchange lewd pictures

rendering the same homage
to an ancient hallowed emblem
as when, high priestess,

I lift the chalice overhead
murmur veneration
and drink the offering

19 Wandering

long lean desert
of desire
freckled brow
sandy hair
sifting through my fingers
lips ardent and inert
smooth rocks of the Mohave
love
your hills roll
down the sheet
your hands   icicle
hold the horizon   within the flames
                        quenching fire
my touch travels   the stalagmite spear
over ridges   melted into metal
over gullies   and the cave is sealed
fingers carve initials under barren ground
on the dunes   while brown weeds
palms open   scatter burrs
downward   the winds
in the pool   fill our footsteps
oasis or mirage   we are lost
odors engulf us
as cactus flowers   River Amazon
bloom   my Mississippi
                        now flow
                        through me
                        across a continent
                        of aching soil
                        erode
                        your Colorado canyon
                        from my palate
                        to the fertile
                        delta
                        of my Nile

20 Pervasion

you sleep
and semen
seeps into the soil
under my rocks and roots
the moisture penetrates

swirls in caverns
oozes over moss
is caught
in turbulent rivers
of the underground

roaring the waters rise
gush throb against the cliffs
cascade in orbits
sink again in eardrums
and subside

slowly the pulsing streams
climb and reach
the forest of my hair
growing thick and green with you
for years to come

21 Come

enter me
blend with me
send healing essence
over my cracks
with your oil
your balm

render my soul intact
drenched by you
cleansed
spread
your unguent
in eddies to mend me

22 End Of The Line

we ban from our bed
anxieties
safe
in arm and leg parentheses

and sink
into sex ecstasy
join raptures
in one exclamation point

punctuating love
to the last dot
but the hour
undoes our body knot

and once more we lie still
in the dark
silent side by side
like question marks

23 Fall

before I snap and flutter off
swathe my skin in rain
polish me with wind
coat me in sunshine varnish
let me sway wide and bright
one last day from your green stem
give me an autumn ecstasy
a final gust of vital energy
before I break my bridle

a sentence to rasp again
until our force is cleaved to silence
triangular larynx leaflet
spread me in a high salute
of grateful homage
once more once more
before our bond is lost
and I spin brown and dry
aimless to solitary white quiescence

Fa is for Mother

24 Free Choice

Pausing in your evening jaunt
on the smooth rim of my kitchen sink
to interrupt my reminiscence
of the tiny perfect infant
I once cradled briefly in one palm,
what are you thinking
as you watch me wash the dishes?

Country spider,
do we all pursue kismetic tracks
or build a random future from each act?
Was my aborted child foredoomed
or victim of haphazard circumstance?
Compare his fate to yours, tonight.

Were you preordained to die
by my hot jet of water on your back
or will your vacant web at dawn
provoke a fresh new series of events
whose consequence may deviate
our planet in its course?
Answer, and I'll spare your life!

But the spider makes no judgement
and so I send him on a scalding wave
into the basin where he spins,
scrambles, clings,
one thin black leg clutching at the grate,
then disappearing
  - also -
down the drain.

25 Fragrance

roses lilacs jonquils honeysuckle
in youthful meditation
her chin upon her knees
she sits inhaling deeply
through garlands on her cotton skirt
her very own plant odor of creation

turned shell from hip to shoulder
galaxies within her grip
she and a man
the universe confined by two bare bodies
and on the final quake of coital power
their blended mineral odor of creation

roses lilacs jonquils honeysuckle
a child rocked in her arms held to her cheek
her nose against the baby's skin
religiously she breathes
pungent and sweet
the infant's animal odor of creation

26 In High Feather

I felt the flutter
of a humming bird
hovering in place
below my waist within
tiny pinions quivering exuberance

then a robin hopping
and the swallow's rise
pressing a blue brow
against my canopy of sky

I felt the wild goose
cruise across the ocean
flapping through dark clouds
through storms
with arrogant endurance

and now one infant eagle soars
wings flung wide and bloody
as it screeches its triumphant anger
in the blaring dawn of birth

27 Reign

I take refuge
in the mountain of my skull
in the marshes of my limbs
prime territory occupied
and from my indigent
periphery
submit to foreign rule

until my battle of revolt
expulses the invader
autonomy reclaimed
and in my arms
a former potentate
clings to the meager booty
of one nipple

28 Maternity

the first time
I was seared with heat
my body held
a ball of fire
the star triumphant
burned its way
out of me
until it rose and blazed
across the sky
I called her Sunshine

the second time
I held the sea
and teamed
with a vast water world
from plankton
to the sharks and whales
out of me
they leapt they flew they sprawled
across the earth
I called him Seagull

the third time
I became a tree
my body twisted
to a bush
an infant from her stem
was plucked
away from me
I saw the open bud
set in my arms
and called her Flower

29 Diapason

From her kitchen window a housewife watches
her black tights prancing on the garden line.
From the radio beside her piano notes cascade
in reckless intervals as they leap haphazardly
then bring themselves to balance
by a perfect pirouette
resolving in the nick of time
as only those of Chopin
can.

With the tips of her toes barely touching the tiles,
she sweeps the riches of her life
from a rainbow sky
and holds its beauty to her breast
in ballerina armloads.
Outside large raindrops spot the stave of steps.

Her stockings kick and skip across the cord.
Upstairs a puppet sits among limp strings
in white pyjamas with black polka dots,
dreaming how he once cavorted
across the foot frame of her little bed,
helter-skelter, on the verge of falling,
retrieving equilibrium
with an exquisite
last-minute arabesque.

Dirty dishes wait in the sink.
The woman plunges her hands into suds of gauze
and smiles as another waltz starts.

30 Heredity

my mother was a mermaid
who left me on a beach
because she was ashamed
of my long legs and feet

I walked to the first village
they said I'd be their queen
because my skin was speckled
because my hair was green

draped in an ermine cape
wearing a jeweled crown
I called to the rolling waves
and threw my scepter down

my mother from the ocean
rose with a school of fish
and paused, her arms flung open
to blow me a mermaid kiss

howling I must be powerful
before diving under the surf
back with two-legged people
I ignored her imperial words

and married a fisherman
instead to make him king
then bore eleven children
five with tails and fins

into the welcoming waters
I tossed my infants home
they burned me as a heretic
a witch, to charcoaled bone

a layer of fine ashes
covers the land and sea
my offspring will hereafter
breathe and swallow me

Sol is for Survivor

31 Celibacy

breasts are knots
and knees apart
evaporate sap
until wood goes rotten
not a single leaf left
to shade the soul
of a great gaunt bone
without marrow

a stiff empty tree
resisting spring
a relic trunk
peeled smooth of its bark
stout calves sawed off
flexed elbows clean
but a patch of parasite moss
at the crotch

when lost in a forest
climb into the hollow
roll into a ball
crush the tree spirit
to a sweet thick powder
otherwise
she's nothing
but a log

32 Libido

card in a pack
I'm flat flat
my world is painted on paper

I run to events
leap forward
and fall out the opposite side

I steal my mother
then destroy the trinkets
as soon as I'm out of the store

I eat my sweet father until I'm ill
then vomit him vomit him
vomit

no Jack can touch me
though I long for his contact
when I'm alone

let him succeed
and clean blood will flow
from the altar of my thighs

how I wish I had strength
to slaughter them all
King Queen and Knave

then brandishing the Ace
rise real and full
with a Joker's smile

33   Litter

into the ocean
if the waves
would seal a surface blemish
and no fish tossed it back onto the coast

or out a window
if like house dust shaken from a mop
it floated off
and no wind coughed its name

or from a bed
if it would melt from head to toe
and sink discreetly through the floor
leaving no stain

or gasoline if I were sure
combustion would be total
no black twin grinning on
after extinction

but if it's left
to lie about
if no municipal disposal booth
announces full recycling

then I suppose the only civil thing
for me to do
is just to leave mine as it is
alive

34 A Meteorite

my children have a game
with a racket they hit a ball
fastened on a long elastic
from a wooden base
into high space
where almost disappearing
it veers
and falls back to the ground

for years I do the same
propel a garish image
to its apogee
the scene receding
to a pinpoint rock
about to cease
until like an enraptured child
I squeal for black relief

but on the edge of night
bound by its leash
the hideous vision turns
and in reverse
careens through peaceful sky
to hurl its impact havoc
yet another time
on memory's cratered earth

35 Via

Under the window of my plane
a continent passes
in patches of land
like the puzzle I had as a youngster
designed to teach State geography.

On a screen of mountains, lakes,
small towns, outlines of great cities,
I project our jumbled history,
scenes I strive to assemble
in mosaic chronology:

first meeting, first phone call,
first kiss, first hotel room,
first coded letter, first chance encounter:
"You, here? What a surprise!"
"Hello. I'd like you to meet my daughter."

Frontier posts I vainly fix
along jungle memory.
After hours of flight,
like a weary kid
who never did know Iowa or Utah's exact place,

abruptly I pour the pieces of our picture
back into its box and shut the lid.
No, this trip I won't contact you.
I quit, too bored, too old,
for any more jigsaw adventure.

36 Da Capo

a monkey scales the wire of its enclosure
squeezes a paw through one tight square
to seize a bag of peanuts
then hangs prisoner on its own fist
unable to retrieve the hard-clutched booty
while a hilarious crowd
watches the bewildered beast
rage and struggle until it drops
and peers past bars at its treasure on the lawn
scooped up by playful spectators
the small net sack refilled
and dangled from the high side of the cage

where the greedy creature climbs
and again is caught
I finally walk on
inwardly shrieking angry zoo words
at this animal and its persistent counterpart
who scampers up the barrier of my mind
and hangs in the same forlorn manner
trapped by the illusion of a loot
too voluminous ever to be pulled
back through the crack
yet after years of humiliating failure
also refuses to understand

happiness means swinging
empty-handed

37 Asunder

I send Fondness to find you.
It journeys over moonlit trails,
not strong enough to climb the peaks
nor leap ravines,
and so at dawn it hobbles home
to whine and yap in failure
at the fence.

I send Desire to find you.
Wild with midnight frenzy,
it flaps about my silent estate,
searching in blatant spirals,
until sunrise
blinds it back to base defeat,
head-down under eaves.

I send Reason to find you.
Fins wave close by.
It swims to the handle of your door,
noses open the panel,
and I hear ocean billows roar,
snore,
between our continental pillows.

38 Ruminant

beneath my teeth
a clitoris
of chewing gum
until spit out
and molded
by a back and forth
routine
between thumb and index
to a penis
finally rolled
into a spiral fetus
and the snails
of stale
aborted children
climb the wall
in rows
above my bed

39 Repose

luckily
the tide goes out at night
the beach lies barren
calm as a cool sheet
waves subside and lap
in a long white line
my pulse ebbs
soft
and phosphorescent

happily
the breakers of the day
that lashed the cliffs
now lick their ragged claws
and I sink into the hush
and lull of patience
as smooth and slow
the ocean rolls in peace
along internal slopes

40   God's Acre

"What do you want done with your body when you die?"
my husband asked and I replied
"I don't care, do what you like with it"
because I knew he couldn't carry my remains
up one of the fierce mountain trails
of a childhood wilderness
and leave it isolated on rough earth to melt
be eaten by the insects and the vultures
bones drying light and porous
scattered by the winds
or by the hooves and paws of roaming beasts

yes, that's how I view my body after death
fertilizer on a rugged slope
until some part of me pulses in deep roots, high leaves
thrashing parched drenched frozen as seasons change
or a savage meal
turning to sleek pungent fur
or feathers on a slashing wing

in lieu of which, I said, "What about you?"
and he described an ancestral burial plot
and orthodox rites

La is for Singer

41 Summit

ascending the ladder rung by rung
out of insanity into the sun
left hand right hand thrust ahead
above is alive, below is dead

the chain can't be broken, huff and heave
the wound is open and so she so she
so she must go up in a long relay
of identical women clawing the clay

anguish engine stoked to the hilt
generating motion, pumping hope from guilt
cells in a hill of termite people
sounds in a strain, her own death rattle

lips of liberty encircle the rim
mouth that will suck her to oblivion
if there is an exit out of the well
a way of transgressing the frontiers of self

a pause, hiatus, one choral sigh
some reward for the terrible tunnel to climb
or will teeth snap shut, bars on a gate
just as she reaches them? no scream no escape

42　Chronic

at a quarter past nine and a quarter to three
time's horizontal, I'm ready to leave
watches are wheels that turn round and round
the hours stretch out, long hands on a dial
flat as a railroad and I'm ready to ride
to step from a platform and travel on

at half-past twelve and six o'clock sharp
vertical time signals me to depart
clocks are tops that spin to a glass
and every instant I'm ready to drink
is a cocktail no one else can mix
a toast to life and then down the hatch

the show will start right on the dot
all of my selves are here on the spot
author and audience waiting with awe
the houselights dim, the curtain rolls back
I step on the stage where I'm ready to act
and bow in the thunder of my applause

at fifteen to nine, at fifteen past three
at noon and at midnight and again at six-thirty
life held in bondage tight as a book
my knees on my forehead I'm bent to a fetus
and all the mysterious minutes between
wait in stiff images for me to look

on each rotation I've heard the knelling
seventy-eight strokes of the bell
strike out the ages, my body unwinds
and spreads and spirals over the face
speared in the navel I'm held in place
I guess I'll be going some other time

43   In Command

junk yard goddess
hammering a crown from jagged cans
setting it with bottle shards
each time I thrust my diadem aside
I chop off the head
of an attendant

junk yard empress
prancing in my royal attire
from barbed wire to barbed wire of the enclosure
incense of ancestors
smoke from rubbish
fills my castle my cathedral

junk yard priestess
born beneath the sign of the phoenix
I arise from every heap of ash
brush the cinders from my hair
and turn fierce beacon eyes
to new horizons

junk yard heiress
finding in a pile of skins
the blackest one that I can wear
zipping it up snug under the chin
to learn by heart
the number on the forearm

junk yard sorceress
I shriek my gibberish to a homeless throng
who scrambles in through one-way gates
to venerate the guttural speech
of their aging
raging hostess

44 Bearings

the weather vane in my blizzard brain
spins madly round
unscrews itself
and falls from reason's spire

hen in the mire
its head cut off
it leaps about the barnyard
in cadence to a rooster's crow

my sorrow goes berserk
and scampers through the forest
seized by hungry elves
who roast it on a bonfire

but when the gnomes begin to eat
seared chicken meat
turns to ash
they spit onto the ground

from cinders and saliva
rises a sublime phoenix
who rushes home
to scale the dome

claws gripping the steeple
it stands erect
and flashes gold and purple sense
its beak piercing the wind

45 Polarity

hemisphere of hope
sunshine and love
sweet cup of warmth and welcome
white note of now
always at the entrance
to a vivid world ahead
we stand with outstretched arms
our ankles in the surf

hemisphere of doubt
of loss of sea
our tangled hair uncut
always at the exit
of a thunder world behind
where each colossal breaker
convulses twenty years
after the flash

bubble of existence
rear of the ears the ocean
and forward
fingers making mountains in fine sand
half obscurity
half radiance
and in between
our globe's filament of spine

46 Encounter

shall we one day stroll again
in royal raiment
along mirrored corridors
execute the graceful minuet
of our embraces
lift full cups of sweet and purple wine
and sup to satiety upon exotic meats
radiant monarchs of our ancient splendor

or meet in the ruins of our domain
forlorn and naked

watching waves caress the banks
sun penetrate snow
roots grip the backs of boulders
raindrops lick the edge of broken panes
in our dismal castle
where we'll lie in separate chambers
longing for the fauna flora jewels and simple elements
we pawned at the height of glory?

who'll make love to us that night
wide awake each on a death bed?

47 Unhallow

I tore your shadow
from under the door
and ripped it to bits
of gaudy confetti
then let great handfuls
fall in a billow
through bars of my skyscraper window

to circle in snow
of lost paper power
filling the air
with a dark bitter cloud
coating your hearse
whose tracks in a row
were traced on wet pavement below

extracting your narrow
mind from the keyhole
I aimed the shaft
straight at your coffin
it hit the lid
and a quivering arrow
transpierced black valentine sorrow

48   Leading Lady

I saw a silly film last night on television
about two women in an automobile collision
who under a scalpel became a single person,
the brain of one transplanted to the other's body.

In the end, Mind's husband accepted the transformation
of his previous blonde mate into a strange brunette
and although his former wife seemed in perfect condition,
Body's ex-husband resigned himself to bereavement.

But I wasn't convinced by this fictive conclusion.
If I were recipient of a similar division:
brain in another body and body with another brain,
Mind's husband would be the widower in mourning,
my wit incapable of mastering new compulsions
when after years of struggle and self discipline
it barely manages to curb old brute sensations.

Flesh would be my domineering factor.
Body's lover would have these same breasts to fondle.
Body's babies their familiar spontaneous protection.
Body's voice might express astounding reflections
with fresh vocabulary but my customary stammer.

49 Token

Cross-legged against a wall
sits a ragged, bearded man
half-way along an underground tunnel
holding out a dark, gnarled hand

not making a second gesture
toward the crowd which bustles by
to dole back gratitude or resentment.
Intrigued, I slow my stride.

His gaze is strange. Both eyes are blue
but in azure of different shades.
Pale, the right shines with approval
like a gentle summer day.

The other, stern, black-spangled,
forebodes winter anger.
Is my next step good or bad?
Subway oracle, I beg for your answer!

How to distinguish weak from kind?
What discriminates cruel from courageous?
I'll fill your cup with all my coins
if you'll wink, once!

50 Joy After Pain

Under Mirabeau bridge flows the Seine.
He recited it over and over again
as we strolled through the city, hand in hand,
until hope faded and dark belfries rang,
bringing us, forlorn exiles, to blink back our tears
and swear we'd never forget these love dreams,

although night descended and a new life came.
Time is long, currents strong, but the girders remain.

During decades I gave him almost no thought,
even when occasionally I chanced to cross
the Mirabeau bridge, yet today I stop
and lean on the ramp at the very spot
where we once stood enlaced, passionately devoted,
and remember the words of the exquisite poem,

before night descended and a new life came.
Out of sight, out of mind, only lyrics remain.

An elderly gentleman at the other end
of the bridge meditates on where it all went.
Is it you, my sole soul mate of a world now past?
What if I approached you and simply asked
if you happen to be the young man I vowed once
to never forget, would you care who I was?

For night descended and a new life came.
The Seine weaving beneath me, alone, I remain.

Si is for Spectator

51 Carolyn's Account

In the garage, she'd grab Dad's yardstick.
In the hall, his ruler.
Neither measured my degree of misbehavior
but depended merely on our location in the house.

In the kitchen, it would be a wooden spoon.
On the veranda, the dog's leather leash.
In the dining room, a large plastic bowl
after she'd dumped the fake fruit on a chair.

In the living room, a thick sash from a drape
with little metal rings sewn at both ends.
In the bathroom, while hers seared my ears,
the damp tongue of a towel lashed my back and legs.

In her room, the flat side of her hair brush.
In mine, my favorite book of fairy tales.
Years later, I heard a woman say
her mother always beat her with a coat hanger.

And I felt a sudden wave of pride.
Had I been loved much more than I suspected?
Never once, not once in all my life,
did my mother strike me with a coat hanger.

52 By Any Other

"Lottie," she said
and a troubled expression
flashed over the young soldier's face
then he gave a brusque nod
sending her back into camp
going she heard
the crackle of guns
as the people behind her were shot

later she marched
on a country road
saw a curve out of view
of the guards at each end of the column
rolled into a ditch at the bend
and lay still in the leaves
while prisoners' feet
pounded past her all day

a coat from a corpse
to cover her forearms
milk from cows in a field
following orders to mute refugees
she trudged many miles in the horde
to a seaport at dawn
where she sneaked clandestine
on a boat

and came to a commonplace land
the horrors of youth
interned in black silence
except for a dream of a soldier her age
who walks from the wire fence
to where she stands shaking
stark naked
and asks for her name

53 Holla

at two in the morning the telephone rang
and over my husband's snoring
came a soft voice
I asked her to wait
groped from the room
closed the door on the cord
sat down in the dark hall and said
"go ahead"

the call was long distance
haphazardly dialed
she wanted simply
to bid someone goodbye
added first name and home town
then taking my silent iteration of facts
for boredom perhaps
she hung up

I phoned the police
who managed to locate the source
notified distant colleagues who saved her
we sent cards at Christmas
later we met
I didn't much like her
nor she, me, I felt
and so that was that

except for faint sobbing
that rings in my head
when I sometimes wake up
in the middle of night
and remember the cold rough wall on my back
and the plea heard from far off
"whoever you are
please listen"

54 Side Light

he was there in sunshine on the screen
a young man leaning over
to embrace his sleeping child
and we were charmed by the scene
on evening news
that we'd zapped to lackadaisically

it isn't often reporters show us
ordinary joy
a father kneeling in a meadow
his infant on his knees
rocking gently as we realize
the man is weeping

the blanket on the body in his arms
a plastic shroud
then other pictures follow
armored cars, devastated buildings
on-the-spot coverage
is the announcer's comment

we turn the TV off
and sit without speaking

55 Advertisement

As I walked down a city street
on my way home one evening,
I saw two posters on a wall.
One showed a cat before a can
of food, its whiskers raised, aloof.
And, on the ad, the caption said:
Titbits To Tempt The Most Disdainful.

Beside it hung another picture
of a starving infant
who squatted naked in the mud.
And on the edges of the sheet
ran letters, spelling out one word.
A tattered boundary, hard to read, repeated:
Hunger Hunger Hunger.

I hurried home, for it was late.
The night air was so chilly.
But finally reaching my front door
I wondered how long it would take
that cat who had too much to eat
to push the extra can of food
to the poor child across the paper.

56   Guilt Trip

the sinners come
in droves across the desert
busloads disembarking
to stand in weary lines outside the gate
some regretting great cruelty
others obsessed by one unintentional absence
or minor mistake
each category of offense
bears its own ticket color
bright Hatred Vengeance Murder
mingle with pale Ingratitude or Rudeness

thus hours pass under zenith heat
pilgrims eager to forget their shame
impatient for admittance
to this redeeming haven
where tears will flow along dark furrows
(as claimed in the brochure)
and moisten roots of jungle plants
whose somber luscious fruit is grown
in order to be plucked by a deserving few
chosen by the hostess of these grounds
for full appeasement

although warned that punishment
for counterfeit remorse
will leave them maimed by monsters
from the underbrush
they push ahead
penetrate the garden
some destined for mutilation
some blessed to swallow Nectar Of Soul Peace
the rest to file back onto buses at nightfall
disgruntled by this grossly over-rated tour
into Repentance

57 Spaceites

I walked across the moon
I was the first man to explore the universe
to leave the traces of my boots
in lunar loam
and lift my eyes to our earth rising
blue balloon

my shadow simian in earthlight
ascended dunes of bone-white dust
had I regressed during the flight
to a missing link?
I leapt in heavy monkey strides
toward border gloom

stepped through jagged fangs of grey
into a murky zone
a horde of phantoms clothed in capes
hid their faces under hoods
I pushed ahead
my torch beam on a group of huddled ghosts

heard them imploring in low moans
that I be gone
let them restore purgatory
on our satellite's lacklustrous side
I explained they must locate
some other somber home

and left
my earphones hummed a message
what was I doing so far from base?
"Return to your place!"
I bounced away from ancestral domains
propelled on hissing specter curses

my colleagues swear they've moved
no astronaut of a subsequent mission
discovered any vestiges
of ancient dwellings for lost souls
they must have migrated
to Neptune

58 Aloof

A Fun Van stands
at the corner of our street.
The driver honks his joyous greeting
and all the children shout and run
scramble on and grin and wave
as the Wonder Bus departs
leaving me behind a tree
alone.

A Marriage Carriage
parks at our curb.
A potential groom comes to my door.
My mother answers she's sorry I'm out.
Cautiously from my room I watch
as my lover returns
to his conjugal hearse
and drives off.

A Train To Fame
huffs at the platform.
An ambitious crowd
surges into the cars
and jams the aisles,
passengers with tickets for Celebrity.
The engine roars past the bench where I sit
in a now empty station.

A Hope Boat whistles
with a forlorn horn.
The wharf swarms with candidates.
Unfortunate people file up the gangplank.
The ship lifts anchor
and steams from the harbor.
In the dark I walk back
to a miserable home.

A Plane To Oblivion
hums on the track.
The hostess motions for me to board
then locks the hatch.
One seat vacant among a group
who smile their warm welcome.
So here I am, at long last
a gregarious member.

59 Radicals

Along the gravel walks,
stalks of gaudy flowers
lift their haughty limbs,
thick with blossoms as large as human faces
and on an equal level.
With root feet firm
in rigid patterns near the paths,
the plants stand regimented,
drilled, restricted,
bound in ground and horticultural good manners,
every leaf respecting its proper slant,
until excessive heat stimulates the stems.
High spirits rock them to revolt.
Tubular toes are torn from soil.

Legions of rioting shrubs
stampede down dusty aisles
and swarm through dark iron gates.
A mob of raucous bushes
cross the boulevard of honking vehicles
and gather on the riverbank beyond
to dance and jubilate along the wharf,
celebrating freedom
in one orgiastic afternoon
and late into the evening,
until the final rebel falls
under the bleaching moon
that cancels red and yellow,
pink and purple petals.

Drab wilted branches lie
in lifeless heaps scooped up at dawn
by municipal street cleaners.
When news comes to the ears
of those docile colleagues who refused
to break the garden rules,
they nod huge blooms
and murmur that they're better off
still living in a formal order,
rather than roaming in a reckless crowd
to inevitable doom,
even though the others surely knew
brief but sublime quintessence of escape
and independence.

60 Deposit

"Yield. Sink." "I do. I drift. I fall."
"Still choosing your direction in the wind!
I want surrender, absolute release,
death of the dreamer, extinction of all light,
a leaf, a piece of bark, swept down the rapids,
stunned silent on the surface of a pond."

"I try. I do my best: chop off my fingers,
break my teeth. I have no tentacular foot
to hold me firm. I'm nothing but an eye
open in a cataract of colors,
a pebble on the mud floor of a lake.
Are you pleased?" "This far, pacified."

61 Crypt

as doors behind slam shut
others swing open
straight ahead
a corridor appears
unsuspected exit
from the present
entrance to the precinct
next in place

as lights go off behind
weird luminescence
burns beyond the bend
of passageways
darkness swallows up
the cold spent moments
novelty irradiates
a sheen

as sounds die out behind
notes of strange music
vibrate from the far end
of a hall
panes of the past lie shattered
in still gravel
chimes of the future
tinkle in a draft

62 Nostalgia

I started as a frozen embryo
then I became one of a hundred clones,
separated from ninety-nine twin brothers,
implanted in a strange surrogate mother.

I grew up to be trained as astronaut
and left a lovely bride to journey off.
When I came back to earth I saw her,
no more my wife but now my great granddaughter.

I'll never figure out my horoscope.
I'm out of pace but is it fast or slow?
I'll return to my native laboratory,
have a computer tell me my life story.

For even though as soon as I was born
they sold me to some wealthy foreigners
I still remember my primeval cluster
of siblings who must be somewhere or other.

My origin's a mystery I'll explore
to learn some anecdotes about my folks,
ascend my family tree till I discover
the source of one frozen
poor orphan
embryo.

The Author . . .

GWYNETH HUGHES studied opera and went to sing in France. There she was stimulated by the culture of the vibrant Parisians, and not content with established theatre roles, she began writing her own serious plays and poetry, which she used with music to create various moods.

Driven by her artistic curiosity, she soon diversified into other media. She put on a show at the Pensée Sauvage with slide projections of paintings accompanied by her own poetry readings. Her success prompted her to put on more audio-visual shows. Now that she had an audience, she experimented further.

She put on light musicals in Paris, but had difficulty finding English-speaking actors/singers to match her scripts. Undeterred, she began giving imaginative one-woman performances and song shows.

The lack of supporting actors further prompted her to use theatrical character dolls, which she designed herself, and slides of these to enlighten her performances. Her performances developed into large screen slide shows with dialogue read by a small group of off-stage actors.

And so she created her own unique, artistic productions, with realistic, thought-provoking and topical themes such as mental illness, prostitution, surrogate mothers, cybernetic lovers, all seen from her highly feminine viewpoint. Her shows blossomed with the introduction of more elaborate costumes and sets.

The continuing success of the verse slide shows of her plays and poems reveal her to her audiences as a lady with truly remarkable artistic talent, who once seen, can never be forgotten.

Readers wishing to communicate with the author about this work, are advised in the first instance, to address their correspondence to Gwyneth Hughes, c/o Pipers' Ash